THE
NBA

A HISTORY OF HOOPS

Published by Creative Education
P.O. Box 227, Mankato, Minnesota 56002
Creative Education is an imprint of The Creative Company
www.thecreativecompany.us

Design and production by Christine Vanderbeek
Art direction by Rita Marshall

Printed by Corporate Graphics in the United States of America

Photographs by Dreamstime (Munktcu), Getty Images (Andrew D. Bernstein/NBAE,
Tim Defrisco, James Drake/Sports Illustrated, Ron Hoskins/NBAE, George Long/Sports
Illustrated, George Long/WireImage, Fernando Medina/NBAE, Layne Murdoch/NBAE,
NBA Photo Library/NBAE, NBA Photos/NBAE, Dick Raphael/NBAE, Rogers Photo
Archive, George Rose, William R. Sallaz/NBAE, SM/AIUEO, Larry W. Smith/NBAE,
Rick Stewart, Terrence Vaccaro/NBAE, Rocky Widner/NBAE, Jeremy Woodhouse),
iStockphoto (Brandon Laufenberg)

Library of Congress Cataloging-in-Publication Data
LeBoutillier, Nate.
The story of the Oklahoma City Thunder / by Nate LeBoutillier.
p. cm. — (The NBA: a history of hoops)
Includes index.
Summary: The history of the Oklahoma City Thunder professional
basketball team from its start as the Seattle SuperSonics in 1967
to today, spotlighting the franchise's greatest players and moments.
ISBN 978-1-58341-962-5
1. Oklahoma City Thunder (Basketball team)—History—Juvenile literature.
2. Basketball—Oklahoma—Oklahoma City—History—Juvenile literature.
I. Title. II. Series.
GV885.52.O37L43 2009   796.323'640976638—dc22   2009035971

CPSIA: 120109 PO1093

First Edition
2 4 6 8 9 7 5 3 1

Page 3: Guard James Harden
Pages 4–5: Forward Nick Collison

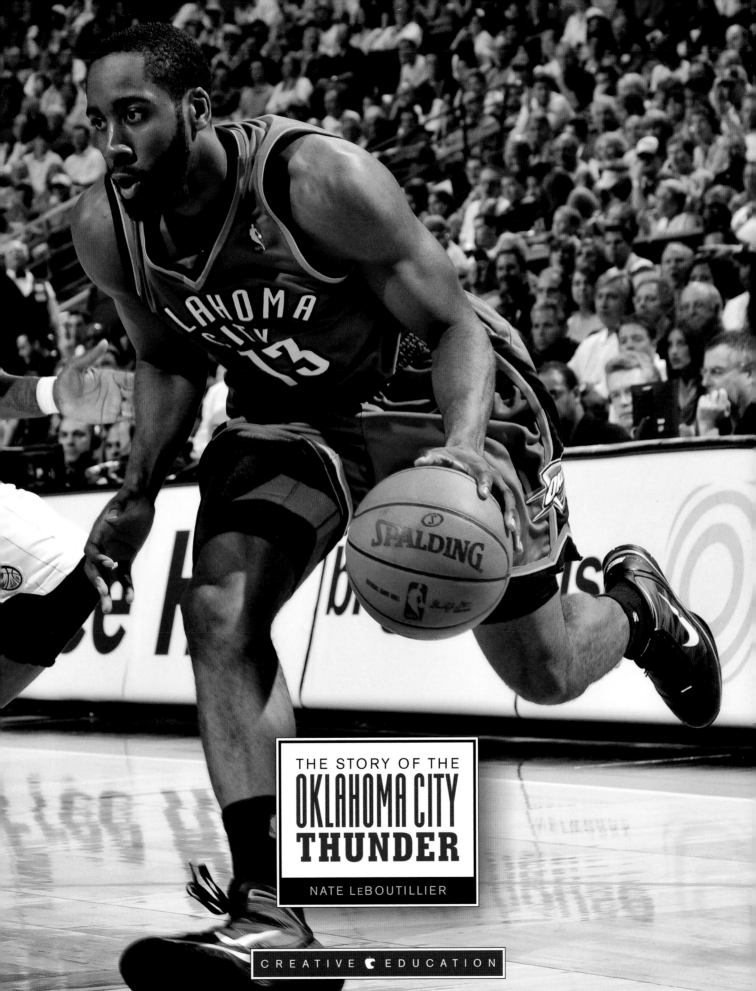

THE STORY OF THE
OKLAHOMA CITY
THUNDER

NATE LeBOUTILLIER

CREATIVE EDUCATION

CONTENTS

CHAPTER ONE

FAR FROM THE PLAINS

On April 22, 1889, Oklahoma City was founded in a single day when some 10,000 pioneering folk descended upon what became the downtown area and set up a "tent city" during the famous Oklahoma Land Run. Eventually, commerce and industry settled in, and the town grew to become the state of Oklahoma's capital and largest city. With a metropolitan area featuring more than one million residents, Oklahoma City stands today as one of the model cities of the American South.

In 2008, another pioneering group settled in Oklahoma City: a National Basketball Association (NBA) franchise called the SuperSonics. Franchise owner Clay Bennett, a native Oklahoman, moved the team from Seattle, Washington, to Oklahoma City after the prospects of making a profit in Seattle turned sour. Soon after, the new residents of Oklahoma City became known as the Thunder—a reference to the storms so common over the state's prairie landscape—and professional basketball in "The Sooner State" was off and running.

Situated on America's plains, Oklahoma City experiences a wide array of weather events, from tornadoes to heat waves to winter storms.

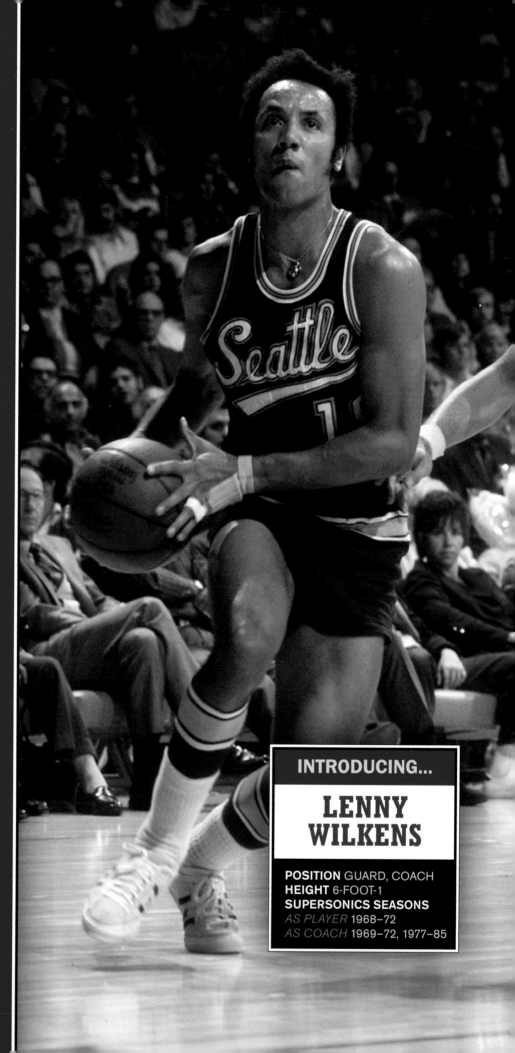

AS A SOPHOMORE AND JUNIOR, LENNY WILKENS NEVER EVEN WENT OUT FOR HIS HIGH SCHOOL BASKETBALL TEAM. He didn't think he was good enough. Luckily for Wilkens—and the rest of the basketball world—a friend convinced the young guard to try out his senior year. The smooth-shooting and slick-passing Wilkens proved a wizard on the high-school court, inspiring team play in much the same way he later would in the NBA. He joined the St. Louis Hawks via the 1960 NBA Draft and led his team to the Finals as a rookie, then was traded to the Sonics in their second season of existence in 1968–69 and averaged 22.4 points per game. His next three seasons in Seattle, Wilkens served as player/coach, and the team improved each year. But the Sonics traded him away, and it would be five seasons before the team welcomed him back as head coach only. In 1979, the SuperSonics, under Wilkens's guidance, won their only NBA title. "I loved that team," Wilkens said. "We believed in ourselves and knew we would find a way to win no matter what. That was special."

INTRODUCING...

LENNY WILKENS

POSITION GUARD, COACH
HEIGHT 6-FOOT-1
SUPERSONICS SEASONS
AS PLAYER 1968–72
AS COACH 1969–72, 1977–85

The history of the Thunder franchise is rooted in Seattle, one of the Pacific Northwest's great cities. In 1967, Seattle—home to the Boeing Company, which builds some of the world's largest jets—was awarded an NBA team and named it the SuperSonics after the powerful aircraft. The SuperSonics' first season ended with a 23–59 record. Forward Walt Hazzard provided plenty of offense, but the Sonics seemed to lack leadership. Seattle solved that problem after the season by trading Hazzard to the Atlanta Hawks for veteran guard Lenny Wilkens.

The trade paid off immediately. In 1968–69, Wilkens finished second in the NBA in assists as Seattle improved its record by seven wins. The next season, Wilkens remained a player but served as the team's coach as well. His calm personality and intelligence made him a great coach, and his speed made him an All-Star player. In 1971–72, Seattle posted its first winning record at 47–35.

Besides Wilkens, part of the reason for Seattle's improvement was Spencer Haywood, an explosive young forward known for his amazing leaping ability and rare shooting touch. "When Spencer was on, he could demoralize the other team single-handedly," explained Sonics center Bob Rule. "He'd pull up from 25 feet and launch one [shot] after another into the rafters. Somehow the ball would usually come down *snap* in the center of the basket."

HAYWOOD'S HARDSHIP

FROM 1971 TO 1975, SUPERSONICS FANS WERE TREATED TO THE HIGH-ENERGY GAME OF FORWARD SPENCER HAYWOOD. After growing up poor in Mississippi, Haywood resolved to make a better way for his family, and in 1969—as a 20-year-old who had played just 2 years of college ball—he signed with the American Basketball Association's (ABA) Denver Nuggets, since the NBA didn't allow underclassmen in its draft. Following a long court battle, Haywood won a legal appeal to enter the NBA and came to Seattle in 1970. This led to the NBA's "hardship rule," which allowed early draft entrance to players who could prove financial hardship. Seattle fans loved Haywood's rim-rocking style, but on the road, Haywood took some verbal abuse from those who thought he didn't yet belong in the league. "I was in the court one day and on the court the next day, and they were booing and throwing bottles at me," he later recalled. Kevin Garnett, the 2004 NBA Most Valuable Player (MVP) and a former "hardship" case himself, thanked Haywood in his MVP acceptance speech, saying, "I'm forever grateful to [him] for leading the way."

Despite Seattle's success, Wilkens was feeling the strain of serving as both coach and starting guard. "I began to realize that I had to do a lot more to coach successfully," he said. Wilkens asked the team to remove coaching duties from his job description, wanting to concentrate solely on his playing career, which he felt could last a few more years. Seattle management listened to Wilkens's thoughtful reasoning ... and then traded him to the Cleveland Cavaliers for young guard Butch Beard. The move backfired. Without Wilkens, the Sonics plummeted to 26–56 in 1972–73.

To steady the team, Seattle brought in former Boston Celtics star center Bill Russell as coach. In only his second season in Seattle, Russell guided the Sonics to a winning record and their first trip to the playoffs. Providing firepower during that 1974–75 season were Haywood and guard Fred Brown, whose long-range bombs earned him the nickname "Downtown" Freddie Brown. Both players averaged more than 21 points per game. "It was interesting, because when I got there, he was on billboards and buses," said Brown of Haywood. "He was Superman of the SuperSonics. I had never seen anything like that. He was the man."

THE AMERICAN BASKETBALL ASSOCIATION CROPPED UP IN 1967 WITH THE PROMISE OF A FREE-WHEELING STYLE OF BASKETBALL AND TICKET OPTIONS THAT WERE MORE AFFORDABLE TO THE AVERAGE FAN THAN THOSE OFFERED BY THE MORE-ESTABLISHED NBA. The ABA incorporated a three-point shot, used a red-white-and-blue ball, and encouraged showmanship and hot-dogging. For nine seasons, the ABA and NBA existed concurrently, and while the ABA was constantly challenging its NBA "big brother" for basketball supremacy, the NBA treated the ABA with more of an "undesirable third cousin" air of disdain. Still, for five seasons, from 1971 to 1975, the NBA accepted the ABA's challenge to play interleague preseason exhibition games. All games were to be played at ABA arenas, since the NBA didn't want the publicity and felt the games were beneath it. That is, all games except one, when the ABA's Indiana Pacers played the NBA's SuperSonics on the Sonics' home court in Seattle on September 28, 1971. For the record, the Sonics mopped up on the Pacers, 117–93. But it is a little-known fact that the ABA won the all-time series versus the NBA, 79–76.

The spark plug that drove the Sonics, though, was Don "Slick" Watts. At a slim 6-foot-1, Watts was known for his uncanny speed and quick hands—and the bright green headband he wore around his bald head. After arriving in 1973, Watts won over Seattle fans with his hustle and community involvement. "In the 10 years of the Sonics, I don't know of one player on a par with Slick Watts as far as desire on the court and ability to make people happy," team owner Sam Schulman once said. "I wish I had 12 Slick Wattses on my team."

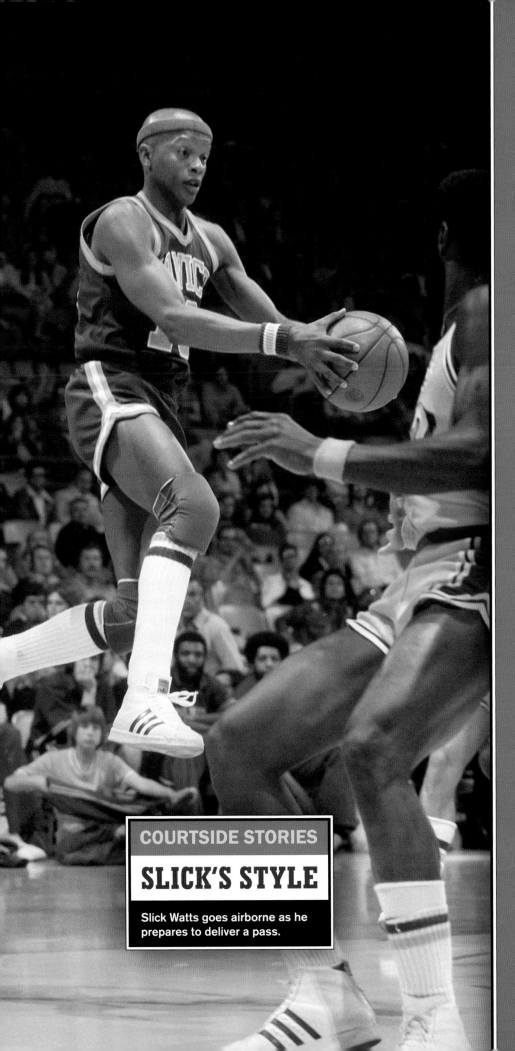

COURTSIDE STORIES

SLICK'S STYLE

Slick Watts goes airborne as he prepares to deliver a pass.

FASHION TRENDS COME AND GO IN THE NBA. Short shorts, long shorts. Afros, cornrows. Tattoos, "air" shoes. One trend has come, gone, and come back again: the headband. Don "Slick" Watts, who played point guard for the SuperSonics for five seasons in the mid-1970s, was one of the first to make headband-wearing fashionable, sporting it cockeyed on his hairless crown. "All these guys wearing headbands now are just following Slick Watts," said John Lucas, a former NBA guard and coach. "But he was more than a guy with a headband. He was a good point guard who really knew how to distribute the ball." Watts's best season was 1975–76, when he averaged 13 points, a league-leading 8.1 assists, and 3.2 steals per game. Although he was traded away to the New Orleans Jazz and missed the Sonics' championship season of 1978–79, Watts returned to the Pacific Northwest and taught physical education in Seattle's schools following his NBA career. "It's good to see the kids come back with the headbands," Watts said. "It lets people know that Slick Watts is still alive."

CHAPTER TWO

WINNING WITH WILKENS

The summer of 1977 was a tumultuous one for Seattle. Haywood, who had often clashed with Coach Russell, was traded away. Other players had also grown tired of Russell's domineering coaching style, so Schulman then forced Russell to resign. Without their star player and respected coach, the Sonics won just 5 of their first 22 games in 1977–78 with an interim coach before asking Lenny Wilkens—now retired as a player—back to coach in a permanent role.

Wilkens quickly reshaped Seattle's lineup, trading away the popular Watts and building around a talented trio of guards. With feisty Dennis Johnson running the point, Brown moved to the bench to become the team's sixth man, and acrobatic guard Gus Williams was inserted into the starting lineup instead. Coach Wilkens also gave bigger roles to Marvin Webster—a 7-foot-1 center known as "The Human Eraser" for his shot-blocking skills—and rookie center Jack Sikma, as well as veteran forward John Johnson.

Nicknamed "The Wizard," Gus Williams was not only an elite scorer but a brilliant defender, ranking yearly among the NBA's steals leaders.

The team had also picked up the ultimate complementary player in Paul Silas in the summer of 1977. The veteran had been a championship-caliber forward with the Celtics in his prime but was now at the tail end of his career. Silas provided great veteran leadership, taking Sikma, especially, under his wing. "Look anywhere on our team and you'll see Paul's influence," said Wilkens.

Fans quickly saw the wisdom of Wilkens's moves when the Sonics won 42 of their final 60 games in the 1977–78 regular season and then roared past two playoff opponents to reach the NBA Finals. It was evident Wilkens was doing something very right. "What did Wilkens have that Russell and [coach Bob] Hopkins lacked?" asked Seattle sportswriter Blaine Johnson. "Maybe more organization, maybe more communication, [or] maybe he wound up with the right blend of personalities. One thing is certain—he put all the necessary ingredients into the pot at the right time."

In the Finals, Seattle faced off against the Washington Bullets, who were led by star center Wes Unseld. The series was an epic battle, but the Bullets won in seven games. Game 7, played in Seattle, was particularly disappointing for the Sonics guards. Williams missed 8 of his 12

FRED BROWN

POSITION GUARD
HEIGHT 6-FOOT-3
SUPERSONICS SEASONS 1971–84

WHEN THE NBA PAINTED A THREE-POINT ARC ON ITS COURTS FOR THE FIRST TIME IN 1979, LONG-RANGE BASKETBALL SHOOTERS EVERYWHERE REJOICED, NOT LEAST AMONG THEM "DOWNTOWN" FREDDIE BROWN. Brown, who had a successful, high-scoring collegiate career at the University of Iowa, was drafted by both the SuperSonics and the ABA's Kentucky Colonels. But he chose the Sonics and became that rare player who spends a long career (13 seasons, in Brown's case) with the same team. Brown, with his trademark goatee and Afro, came off the bench as a sixth man for much of his pro career, and by 1978–79, the year the Sonics won the only championship in franchise history, Brown was considered such an integral part of the squad that he was named team captain. The 14 points per game he averaged that season didn't hurt, either. Upon retirement from the NBA, Brown went into banking but remained in Seattle. "The city still cherishes our championship," Brown said. "When I'm out and about, I hear the constant chatter of, 'Get back in the game, Fred.'"

shots, and Dennis Johnson, appallingly, missed all 14 of his. Despite

this poor showing, the Sonics lost only by a 105–99 score, leaving

Seattle fans to wonder, "What if?"

Although dispirited, the Sonics vowed that they would be back, and

they spent the 1978–79 season fulfilling that vow. Manning the

forward positions were Lonnie Shelton—the team's enforcer—and

John Johnson, and Sikma controlled the pivot. Williams and Dennis

Johnson continued to form a magnificent guard duo, and Brown and

Silas provided great bench support. Together, these players formed

the "Seattle Seven." After a 52–30 season, Seattle tore through the

playoffs to face the Bullets again in the NBA Finals.

After losing to the Bullets 99–97 in Game 1 in Washington, D.C.,

Seattle proved unstoppable for the rest of the Finals. The Sonics

destroyed the Bullets four games to one, bringing Seattle its first NBA

championship. Williams averaged nearly 30 points per game in the

series, and Dennis Johnson, who was all over the floor for Seattle,

won the Finals MVP award, avenging his horrible performance in the

previous year's final game. "Last year we didn't know what to expect in

this series, but we came in with our eyes open this time," said Johnson.

"We did everything we had to do to win."

The victory was particularly sweet for Wilkens, who—before he would retire from coaching—would become the NBA's all-time leader in coaching victories yet win just the one championship, with Seattle. "I still remember when I took over that team," Wilkens later recalled with a laugh. "I had heard general managers and other people say it was the worst team ever. And when I turned them around, all of a sudden everyone said, 'Well, we all knew they had the talent.'"

The next season, Seattle fans watched their club achieve its best record yet, 56–26, with the core of its championship team intact. But a new Western Conference foe, the Los Angeles Lakers, had risen to power behind center Kareem Abdul-Jabbar and precocious rookie point guard Magic Johnson. The Lakers whipped the Sonics in the 1980 Western Conference finals, four games to one.

THAT '70s RERUN

Veteran Paul Silas in action during the 1979 NBA Finals.

THE SONICS MADE THE NBA FINALS THREE TIMES
IN THEIR HISTORY, AND TWICE THEIR CHAMPION-
SHIP OPPONENT WAS THE WASHINGTON BULLETS.
In back-to-back years, 1978 and 1979, the green-
and-gold Sonics, with their strong backcourt, met the
red-white-and-blue Bullets, with their strong frontcourt.
Fittingly, each team garnered one championship trophy

out of the deal. The first go-round, the series was an
epic battle that spanned seven games. The Sonics
lost Game 7 more than the Bullets won it as Seattle's
guards shot horribly, leaving Seattle fans with a bitter
taste in their mouths. "That first year, we were just over-
matched," said Sonics coach Lenny Wilkens. "Washington was big, strong, and smart, and they wore us down.

The next year, however, we learned how to play them
and had the type of team that could better deal with the
things they did." Sure enough, the second time was a
charm for Seattle, as it lost Game 1 but won the next
four straight to claim victory. Said Bullets guard Bernie
Bickerstaff, "They were just better than we were the
second time. They were hungry, and they played like it."

The SuperSonics' 1980–81 season was a disaster. The veteran Silas retired, the high-scoring Williams got into a contract dispute that led him to sit out the entire season, and the rough-and-tumble Shelton was shelved by injuries most of the year. To top it off, the Sonics had traded Dennis Johnson, the hero of their lone championship, before the season to the Phoenix Suns for aging guard Paul Westphal. Although many fans had heard of Johnson's moody ways, he was only 25 years old, with his best seasons still ahead of him.

The trade did not pan out well for the Sonics. Although Westphal averaged a respectable 16.7 points a night, he played in just 30 games as the Sonics went 34–48 and missed the playoffs, while Johnson led a successful Suns outfit in scoring and steals. Williams rejoined the team in 1981–82, and the Sonics made it to the second round of the Western Conference playoffs before losing to the San Antonio Spurs.

The Sonics made the playoffs the next two seasons but did no damage there. The popular Brown retired after the 1983–84 season, and Williams was traded to the Bullets at the same time. Sikma, the last remaining member of the Seattle Seven, would finally be traded away in 1986.

INTRODUCING...

JACK SIKMA

POSITION FORWARD / CENTER
HEIGHT 6-FOOT-11
SUPERSONICS SEASONS 1977–86

THE 1979 NBA CHAMPION SUPERSONICS HAD A SQUAD THAT FEATURED LEGENDARY GUARDS AND AN UNSELFISH ATTITUDE. But their man in the middle, Jack Sikma, also played an integral role in bringing home the title. Sikma played his college ball at Division III school Illinois Wesleyan University, where he got little attention but lots of time on the court to develop his game. By his senior season, pro teams were clamoring for his services, and the Sonics nabbed him with the eighth overall pick in the 1977 NBA Draft. In Sikma's second year, Seattle won it all, but Sikma continued to excel for the Sonics for another seven seasons before playing his last five years with the Milwaukee Bucks. Afterward, he began coaching at different levels, working his way up to assistant status in the NBA. "I really enjoy evaluating a player and his skills—what areas do you think he could add, what areas could be a strength for him," said Sikma, an assistant coach with the Houston Rockets in 2009–10. "I like the puzzle and working through the puzzle. That's what coaching is."

CHAPTER THREE

THE X-MAN COMETH

In 1985, the Sonics made Lenny Wilkens a team executive and replaced him as coach with Bernie Bickerstaff. Seattle soon featured a new, exciting collection of players, too. Forward Tom Chambers impressed fans with his scoring and spectacular dunks, guard Nate McMillan emerged as the team's defensive stopper, guard Dale Ellis gave the Sonics lethal three-point shooting, and 6-foot-10 forward Derrick McKey added versatility.

Another new Seattle star was Xavier McDaniel. The fourth overall pick of the 1985 NBA Draft and a fan favorite, "The X-Man" was a skilled rebounder and scorer at the forward position, and a head-shaven intimidator in the paint. "People always say [Chicago Bulls guard] Michael Jordan started the look, and I just laugh," said McDaniel of his trendsetting ways. "Actually, I started the bald head. Slick Watts was the first guy in the NBA to do it, but he was long retired when I arrived. It became my trademark, and then it became everyone's trademark, and I almost had to grow an Afro back."

A 1988 NBA All-Star, forward Xavier McDaniel aimed to create a fear-some image by shaving not only his head but his eyebrows as well.

Although the Sonics' 1985–86 season was a losing endeavor that ended 31–51, it was notable for featuring one of the strangest postponements in sports history. On January 5, 1986, the Suns were in town to play the Sonics at the Seattle Center Coliseum, but in the second quarter, with the Suns ahead 35–24, a crack in the roof let in a Seattle tradition: rain. Puddles formed on the court, and the game had to be rescheduled for the next day. The Sonics went on to win the NBA's only rain delay, 117–114.

In 1986–87, the Sonics posted a 39–43 record during the regular season but sneaked into the playoffs as the seventh seed. Seattle shocked its first-round opponent, the Dallas Mavericks, three games to one, then upended the Houston Rockets in the second round, four games to two. "Bernie had us believing that if we walked in fire, we would come out fine, with no scratches," said McDaniel. Although the Lakers swept the Sonics in the Western Conference finals, high-level basketball seemed to be back in Seattle.

In 1988, Seattle added muscular power forward Michael Cage to its lineup and promptly posted its first winning record in four years. Even though two mediocre seasons followed, two more rising stars emerged: highflying forward Shawn Kemp and multitalented point guard Gary

Payton. Kemp had jumped directly from high school to the NBA, joining the Sonics in 1989 at the age of 19. With his long arms and explosive vertical leap, "The Reign Man"—a pun on Seattle's rainy weather—thrilled local fans with an array of rim-rattling slams.

Payton, meanwhile, quickly earned a reputation around the league for two things: tenacious defense and trash talking. He was quick, but he was also incredibly strong for his size. Nicknamed "The Glove" because he covered his man as tightly as a glove fits on a hand, Payton played suffocating defense and burned with intensity. Away from the court, however, Payton showed a softer side by creating his own charity— the Gary Payton Foundation—to help underprivileged children.

In 1992, George Karl was hired as Seattle's new head coach, and in 1993–94, with a refurbished Key Arena to call home, the Sonics posted an NBA-best 63–19 record. German forward Detlef Schrempf and

INTRODUCING...

NATE McMILLAN

POSITION GUARD, COACH
HEIGHT 6-FOOT-5
SUPERSONICS SEASONS
AS PLAYER 1986–98
AS COACH 2000–05

AS A HEADY BACKUP GUARD, NATE McMILLAN WON OVER MANY SONICS FANS WITH HIS INTELLIGENT PLAY AND RUGGED DEFENSE. Affectionately known as "Mr. Sonic," McMillan played out all 13 of his NBA seasons in Seattle and then began coaching the team immediately after his playing career ended. For two years, he learned the coaching ropes as a Sonics assistant, and by the beginning of the 2000–01 season, he was head coach. The Sonics made the playoffs twice in McMillan's five-year tenure as head coach, but when it came time to lock him up with a new contract in 2005, the Seattle front office balked, and McMillan slipped away to coach for the Portland Trail Blazers, just to the south, down Interstate 5. "This was the time for me to move on," said McMillan. "I needed a different challenge, a different opportunity." Many fans called Mc-Millan's move the beginning of the end for basketball in Seattle, and they may have been right. Bob Weiss was hired as McMillan's replacement in 2005–06 but was fired just 30 games into the job. The Sonics left Seattle for Oklahoma City in 2008.

NICKNAMED "THE GLOVE" FOR HIS ABILITY TO SEEMINGLY FIT RIGHT ON TOP OF THE OPPONENT HE WAS GUARDING, GARY PAYTON WAS THE FLOOR GENERAL FOR MANY SUCCESSFUL SONICS TEAMS THROUGHOUT THE 1990S. Tall and wiry for a point guard, Payton's game was hounding his man and getting steals on defense and then either setting up teammates with nifty passes or taking it to the hole himself on offense. He wasn't a bad shooter, either; in 1999–2000, he led the NBA in three-pointers made with 177. As of 2010, Payton was the only point guard in the history of the NBA to win the Defensive Player of the Year award, which he did in 1995–96. "You think of guys with great hands," said Kevin Johnson, a rival point guard who played for the Phoenix Suns. "Gary is like that. But he's also a great individual defender and a great team defender. He has all three components covered. That's very rare." Payton played for four different teams at the end of his career, winning a championship as a backup with the Miami Heat in 2005–06.

INTRODUCING...

GARY PAYTON

POSITION GUARD
HEIGHT 6-FOOT-4
SUPERSONICS SEASONS 1990–2003

sleepy-eyed forward Sam Perkins added veteran intelligence and excellent outside shooting, but it was the talented Payton–Kemp combination that led the way. "They've always been the two young guys," said Coach Karl. "Now they've blossomed into perennial All-Stars."

But postseason success eluded the top-seeded Sonics when they were shocked by an eighth-seeded Denver Nuggets squad and its young center, Dikembe Mutombo, in the opening round of the 1994 playoffs. The defeat was most bitter, as it was the first time in NBA playoffs history that an "eight" had defeated a "one."

Forward Shawn Kemp took an aggressive approach to playing defense, finishing three NBA seasons as the league leader in personal fouls.

CHAPTER FOUR

ANOTHER FINALS RUN

In 1995–96, the Sonics rebounded gallantly from their crushing 1994 playoff loss. After powering their way to a franchise-best 64–18 record and the Western Conference championship, they met the 72–10 Chicago Bulls—owners of the greatest single-season record in league history—in the NBA Finals. Although Seattle won two games, star guard Michael "Air" Jordan led Chicago to the championship. "Look, we got this far, and a lot of people didn't expect that," said Seattle guard Hersey Hawkins. "A lot of people didn't think we'd beat the Bulls in one game."

In 1997, Seattle traded Kemp away for forward Vin Baker. Even though Baker was not as spectacular an athlete as Kemp, he filled the Sonics' needs. "What we've got from Vin is more versatility, cleverness, backdoor lobs, and spins," said Coach Karl. "There's more variety." Baker teamed up with Payton to lead the Sonics to another great record (61–21) in 1997–98. But Seattle fans were left disappointed as the team bowed

Vin Baker made a splash in his first Sonics season, averaging 19.2 points and 8 boards a night, but he would never again reach those numbers.

out in the second round of the playoffs. Despite having led the Sonics to seven straight winning seasons, Coach Karl was then fired for his inability to bring home an NBA championship.

Former player Nate McMillan took over as Seattle's coach in 2000. McMillan relied on the veteran Payton to guide the Sonics on the court until The Glove was traded to the Milwaukee Bucks for shooting guard Ray Allen in 2003. The 2002–03 Sonics finished 40–42. It was the club's first losing record in 16 years.

But in 2004–05, the Sonics bounced back, exceeding expectations with an impressive work ethic. Behind the play of the high-scoring Allen, explosive forward Rashard Lewis, locally grown point guard Luke Ridnour, and rebounding workhorse Reggie Evans, the Sonics won the Northwest Division with a surprising 50–32 record. In the playoffs, they beat the Sacramento Kings in the opening round before falling to the eventual league champion Spurs.

Unfortunately, this run of success was short-lived. The Sonics fell into a rut for the next three seasons, posting losing records and, worse, losing fan support. It got so bad that new owner Clay Bennett, an Oklahoma City native, made public the idea of moving the team from Seattle to his home city. The winds of change were beginning to blow in Washington.

Even though Ray Allen's greatest claim to fame was his phenomenal three-point accuracy, he was more than capable of scoring inside, too.

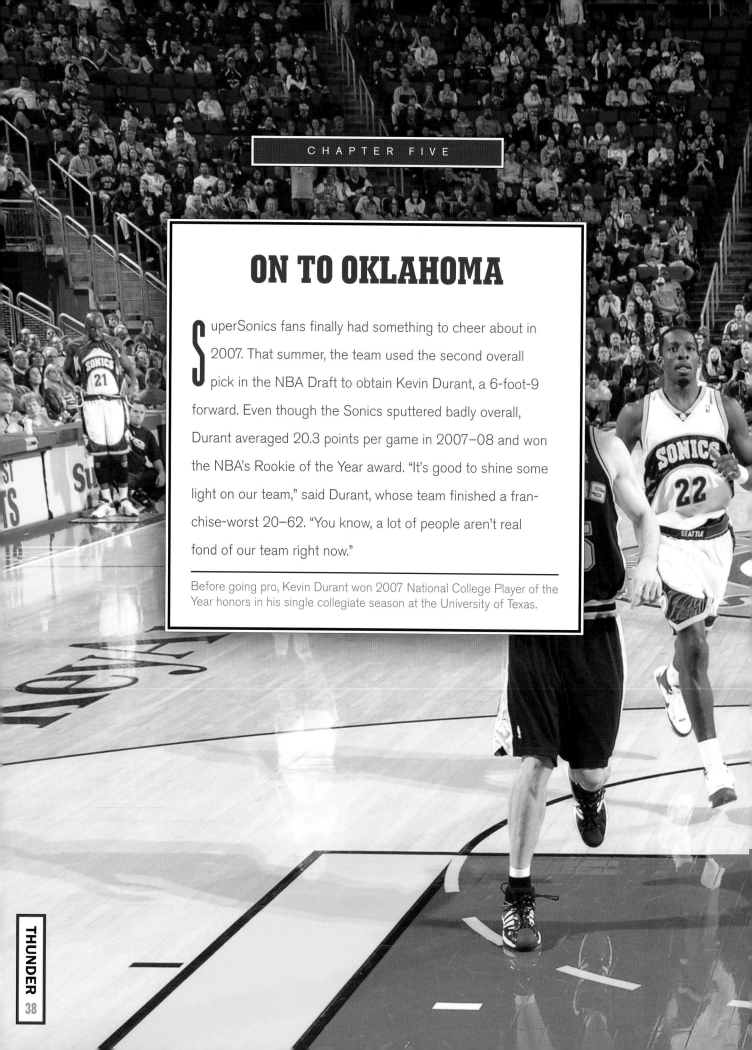

CHAPTER FIVE

ON TO OKLAHOMA

SuperSonics fans finally had something to cheer about in 2007. That summer, the team used the second overall pick in the NBA Draft to obtain Kevin Durant, a 6-foot-9 forward. Even though the Sonics sputtered badly overall, Durant averaged 20.3 points per game in 2007–08 and won the NBA's Rookie of the Year award. "It's good to shine some light on our team," said Durant, whose team finished a franchise-worst 20–62. "You know, a lot of people aren't real fond of our team right now."

Before going pro, Kevin Durant won 2007 National College Player of the Year honors in his single collegiate season at the University of Texas.

lay Bennett's flirtations with relocation turned to reality when, in 2008, Washington lawmakers refused to finance a new arena for the Sonics, who were losing money due to a decrease in attendance at home games. "It gets down to a fairly simple notion," Bennett said. "A private investment demands a return, and this investment will not provide a return."

In July 2008, it was officially announced that the Sonics were leaving Seattle for Oklahoma City. Subsequently, Oklahoma City sped up its process of preparing to host an NBA team, which the city had done in a temporary capacity in 2005–06 and 2006–07 when the local Ford Center hosted the New Orleans Hornets, who had been displaced by the Hurricane Katrina disaster of 2005. As the franchise prepared to start a new chapter, a new name was chosen: the Thunder. New uniforms were also designed, and new season tickets were sold as the team prepared to acclimate to a new home.

WHEN HURRICANE KATRINA RAVAGED THE CITY OF NEW ORLEANS IN AUGUST 2005, NEIGHBORING COMMUNITIES WERE CALLED ON FOR HELP, AND ONE OF THE CITIES ANSWERING THE CALL WAS OKLAHOMA CITY. Due to massive damage, New Orleans Arena would not be able to host the New Orleans Hornets' home games, posing the immediate question, "Where will the Hornets play?" Cities suggested in addition to Oklahoma City included Baton Rouge, Kansas City, Louisville, Nashville, and San Diego. After some deliberation, Hornets owners decided on Oklahoma City, largely because Oklahoma City featured the 19,675-seat Ford Center. The Hornets played 35 of their home games in 2005–06 in Oklahoma City, with the other 6 played in other venues. The arrangement worked out so well for the Hornets that they stayed in Oklahoma City for the 2006–07 season while New Orleans recovered. Following the Hornets' return to New Orleans in 2007, NBA commissioner David Stern deemed Oklahoma City NBA-ready should the league expand or a team want to relocate, announcing, "I can say without reservation that Oklahoma City is now at the top of the list."

WHEN OKLAHOMA CITY BUSINESS-MAN AND SEATTLE SUPERSONICS OWNER CLAY BENNETT GOT THE OKAY FROM THE NBA AND FEDERAL JUDGES TO MOVE THE TEAM TO HIS HOMETOWN IN APRIL 2008, THE CITY OF SEATTLE RETAINED RIGHTS TO THE "SUPERSONICS" NAME AND THE TEAM COLORS OF GREEN AND GOLD. That meant that Bennett's team spent some time as "the yet-to-be-named Oklahoma City team." Proposed names included Wind, Barons, Marshalls, Energy, and Bison. Finally, on September 3, 2008, the new name and colors were announced. The team would be called the Thunder, and its new colors would be blue, orange-red, and yellow. "There's just all kinds of good thunder images and thoughts, and the in-game experience of Thunder," Bennett said. "It's very powerful." Players modeled the new uniforms as some 200 fans showed up to a downtown office building where the team was headquartered. "I love 'em," said coach P. J. Carlesimo. "The biggest mistake you can make with uniforms is going crazy with too much detail. We talked about respecting the heritage of the NBA, and I think we did it."

COURTSIDE STORIES

CALLING DOWN THUNDER

The Thunder's mascot, Rumble the Bison, leads the cheers.

The Thunder's top pick in the 2008 NBA Draft was guard Russell Westbrook, a talented and versatile playmaker at both ends of the court. Although boisterous, appreciative crowds showed up at the Thunder's home games, Westbrook and his teammates started the 2008–09 season by losing 12 of their first 13 contests. As a result, head coach P. J. Carlesimo was fired and replaced by interim coach Scott Brooks. "We have to get better no matter who the coach is," said Durant. "To start off like we did my first year and now this year is tough to deal with. If we continue to work hard, things will start to turn around for us."

Durant was right. Under Coach Brooks's direction, the team's play improved as young stars Durant, Westbrook, and forward Jeff Green redoubled their work efforts and began playing with more cohesion. The midseason acquisition of young center Nenad Krstic gave the Thunder a reliable man in the middle, and by late in the season, the Thunder were giving opponents trouble, even if their final 23–59 record didn't necessarily reflect success. With brawny rookie guard James Harden added to the mix, and with Durant rising to superstar status by netting an NBA-high 30.1 points per game, Oklahoma City continued its ascent in 2009–10. The Thunder made the playoffs, then put up a fight against the defending champion Lakers, losing the series four games to two.

INTRODUCING...

KEVIN DURANT

POSITION FORWARD
HEIGHT 6-FOOT-9
**SUPERSONICS /
THUNDER SEASONS**
2007–PRESENT

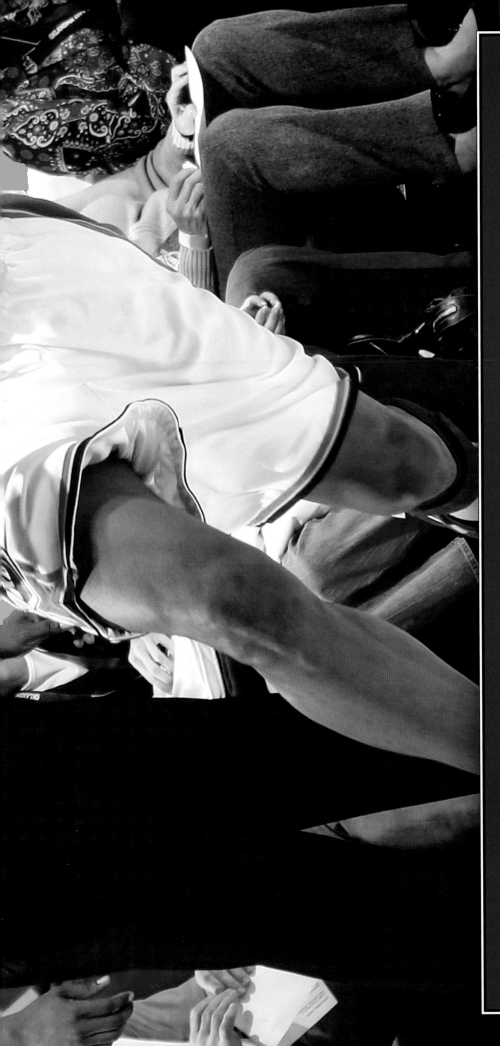

THUNDER FANS QUICKLY GREW FOND OF LANKY, SWEET-SHOOTING FORWARD KEVIN DURANT IN HIS FIRST SEASON IN OKLAHOMA CITY. It was no wonder, since Durant could score from both inside and out and was a virtual bucket-filling machine. But the beginning of Durant's career as a basketball player occurred far away, in the town of Capitol Heights, Maryland, at the Seat Pleasant Activity Center. Durant would go there early mornings to hone his game against older, more physical players. He had many coaches early on who pushed him, too, especially Taras Brown, who led the young Durant through workouts, and, often, to a place called Hunt's Hill. When Durant didn't perform as Brown required, he would make the youngster sprint up steep Hunt's Hill and then backpedal down, often as many as 25 times. Sometimes, he'd let Durant rest at the top of the hill, where one could see the domes and beauty of the nation's capital, Washington, D.C.

"He wouldn't quit," Brown said of Durant. "I would give Kevin days off, and he'd show up at the rec. He wanted to live in the gym."

Although the Thunder franchise's roots will always be Seattle green, the "new" team in orange and blue is planning to make some noise in the NBA's newest market. With a new identity, an exciting core of players, and a fan base thrilled to become a part of the NBA, the rumble of the Oklahoma City Thunder might soon roll across the basketball landscape.

Playing alongside star Kevin Durant, Jeff Green (below) and Russell Westbrook (opposite) took their games to new levels in 2009–10 as the Thunder made a run at the Northwest Division crown.

INDEX